Thank you

Mom

by
Marianne Richmond

Thank you Mom

Marianne Richmond Studios, Inc.
3900 Stinson Boulevard NE
Minneapolis, MN 55421
www.mariannerichmond.com

ISBN 10: 1-934082-21-X
ISBN 13: 978-1-934082-21-8

Illustrations by Marianne Richmond

Book design by Sara Dare Biscan

Printed in China

First Printing

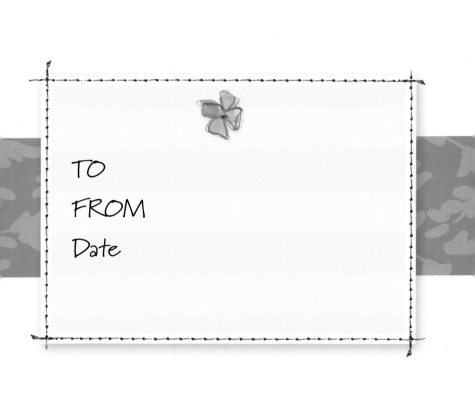

TO

FROM

Date

Dear Mom,

For all the ways you
have shown love to me...

I want to thank you.

Thank you, mom, for always being there.

Twenty-four hours a day, seven days a week.

Whatever

my mood.

Thank you for your nurturing
when I was just a little person...

Thank you for your hours of
rocking,
feeding,
cuddling,
consoling...

and for your protection as
I explored my new world.

Thanks especially for
hanging in there
    when I was having
"one of those days"...

        seemingly every day.

Thank you for growing with me.

For taking time to laugh, talk, play
and be silly with me.

Thank you for nourishing
my body and mind.

And for
teaching my heart about
integrity,
empathy,
kindness
and
gratitude.

Thank you
for affirming
that I am
perfectly perfect
as me.

Thank you, too, for gently
explaining that not everyone
will like or agree with me.

And that that's okay because
God made me to be exactly
who I am.

Thank you for enduring
my phases...

whether it be

music

or

clothing

or

hair color

or

friendships.

Thank you for supporting me through my awkward stage.

Thank you for driving me

to and from... well,

just about everywhere.

Thank you for
encouraging me to
go into the world
and try things...

even if you might have predicted
the outcome.

You know that
confidence and strength
are born amidst the
struggles and disappointments.

And that the greatest gift
is the journey.

Thank you for being home base for my heart...

the person I can go to when I am over-the-moon with joy...

Or when I
feel disappointed,
broken hearted
or just
plain tired
of being a
"grown-up
in progress."

Thank you

for your

gentle wisdom.

Listening ears.

And healing hugs.

Thank you for your prayers.

Thank you for loving me
through times when
I was <u>not</u> as nice
as I could be...

And for
graciously
forgiving me.

Thank you for teaching me
to take care of others in my life.
And for sharing with me
that the secret to happiness is
bringing joy to others.

Thank you, mom,
for caring deeply about me,
day after day,
to this moment in time.

Thank you
for being proud
of me

and for
celebrating me.

Thank you for
being my coach,
counselor,
confidante,
cheerleader,

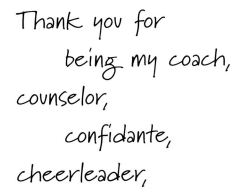

and loyal friend.

I love you,
and I deeply
appreciate
all you have
done for me.

A gifted author and artist, Marianne Richmond shares her creations with millions of people worldwide through her delightful books, cards, and giftware.

To learn more about Marianne's products, please visit www.mariannerichmond.com.